I Now Pronounce You...

NOT GUILTY

ARMAND DELLA VOLPE

BOOMERANG
PRODUCTIONS

I Now Pronounce You...Not Guilty!
Armand Della Volpe
Boomerang Productions

Published by Boomerang Productions, Casselberry, Florida

Cover and Interior design: Davis Creative, DavisCreative.com

Library of Congress Cataloging-in-Publication Data
Library of Congress Control Number: 2019911572
Armand Della Volpe
I Now Pronounce You...Not Guilty!
ISBN: 978-0-692-98407-9
Library of Congress subject headings:

1. SEL023000 SELF-HELP / Personal Growth / Self-Esteem
2. SEL036000 SELF-HELP / Anxieties & Phobias
3. SEL016000 SELF-HELP / Personal Growth / Happiness

2019

Published in the U.S.A.

Dedication

I dedicate this book to my amazing parents, Armand (Del) and Elida Rae (Topaz) Della Volpe, and to Angelina, my life-partner, healer, teacher, lover and bride.

To my daddy, who had no idea he would end up having custody of 4 children; yet managed to commit fully to doing whatever needed to be done to take care of us. During my brief 20 years with him, I always knew he would do all he could to make sure my physical, playful and financial needs were met. He taught me to have as much fun in every moment as one could possibly have. He also inspired my love of nature, amusement parks and theme parks.

To my mama, who just wasn't cut out to be a mother; yet time and time again, she got back on the horse, and brought us back into her home and life regardless of how it would complicate things for her, and hinder her primary love of freedom. She taught me that people do the best they can. She believed in my music and ministry like no other, and considered me her Spiritual teacher. I had her with me for 44 years, and during the last ten years of her life, she became my best friend, which was much more natural to her than motherhood. Through her commitment to making amends to me for her part in our troubled past, I began to feel what unconditional love and forgiveness was all about.

And to my beloved bride, who has been nudging me for years to put my thoughts and feelings into words on paper. She calls me the Goofball Guru and herself the Dingy Devotee and has been writing down things I say for many years. She believed in me when I didn't, and inspired and mirrored so much of what is contained on these pages. She supported me through my many ups and down, and truly proved to me that I was worthy of committed love. She even stayed with me as I navigated through the waters of "love addiction" and depression.

"Angelina…I plan to have a one night stand with you, for the rest of my life."

Table of Contents

SECTION VI

PROLOGUE

Introduction

"We teach best what we most need to learn"
-Richard Bach

My desire for writing this book is to share the tools and experiences that have helped to free me and countless others from the prison of our own psyches as well as inspiring us all to recognize our divine birthright of Peace, Happiness and Contentment. In my 20 years of professional inspirational speaking and musical performances, I have found a common denominator in humanity to be; **the compulsion to feel unlovable**. I also have noticed what all my favorite teachers have, as a cornerstone of their teachings, is to remind us of our inherent beauty, worthiness and **innocence**.

In addition to sharing my own gifts, I will also be referencing my favorite and most powerful practices from dozens of teachers, healers and writers from my last 35 years of spiritual awakening and personal transformation. Of all my talks over the years, this subject has been the most helpful to my audiences and the most important message for me. Join me now on this sacred journey as I make the case for our true eternal innocent nature. Sharing this information is my **community service**.

Throughout the book, I will be using many names for Spirit, like God, Universe, Creator, Divine Presence, Higher Power, etc. Feel free to substitute whatever works best for you.

SECTION I

Calling the Prosecution to the Stand

CHAPTER ONE

Imposed Guilt

"How can we heal the mental disorders of society unless we open our hearts compassionately to the parts of us that are hurting the most?"
-Carl Jung

I was four years old when my parents divorced and my mom went away. At that time I imagined that I must have done something wrong and that I was not unconditionally lovable and safe. This was the beginning of my relationship with guilt but it certainly didn't stop there. Throughout my childhood, I would hear what a good boy I was as well as what a bad boy I was, depending upon whether or not the adults were inconvenienced. Again, I interpreted this as; ***I was lovable when I was good, but unlovable when I was bad.*** I was proud of myself when I was praised, and I felt shameful when I was scolded. I would eventually come to find out that pride and shame were flip sides of the same coin, and I would dance with them throughout my life. In fourth grade, I was diagnosed with *anxiety disorder.* The doctor recommended "Ritalin", but my parents declined.

At an early age, I also began to go to church as well as Catechism and Vacation Bible School. I don't know about you, but one of the first things I remember learning in church was, "You were born of original sin." Wow! Here I am at a place that is supposed to help me have a relationship with God and/or my own Higher Power, and that's what my trusting ears hear. Dr. Phil would ask, "How's that working for ya?" Instead of being guided to feel safer, more connected and lovable, most of us ended up feeling less worthy and guilty for our existence. Our parents, childhood teachers and peers continued to add their fuel to the fire. Anytime anyone expressed disappointment in us or anger towards us, we added that to our guilt stockpile and felt less lovable.

Throughout our lives, we have been relentlessly bombarded by the outside world with tons of affirmations that there is something wrong with us, and our lovability is completely conditional. Actually, "conditional love" is an oxymoron since love is by its very nature, unconditional. Years later, I heard and realized that we were actually "born as an original blessing." This rings much truer to our hearts and souls, but unless we remove the shackles of our imposed guilt and heal the wounds of our well-meaning parents, teachers and peers, our unconscious shame will ultimately run the show.

If it were only outside forces that were inspiring us to feel that we are not enough, I believe that we would be much more able to combat those forces with our conscious thoughts. The bigger challenge is that all of those negative affirmations go into our subconscious thoughts and become a part of our psyche. Unlike the TV and other external voices and images, it is much more challenging to turn off the voices in our heads, which run 24 hours a day. I will discuss more on that later, but you are getting an idea of what we are dealing with here. Much of this book will be devoted to reminding us of whom we REALLY are and refusing to entertain any external or internal concepts that would have us believe otherwise. Our true Self is an eternal, innocent, divine, spark of Light. You can call this God, Source or otherwise: it really doesn't matter. When we truly embrace this Knowing, our lives will reflect that Knowing, and Peace and Joy will inevitably flow through every aspect of our lives.

CHAPTER TWO

Confessing To a Crime We Didn't Do

"It is so tempting to judge ourselves and others but that doesn't make it any less destructive."
-Goofball Guru

Many years ago, Angelina and I were watching an Oprah show. Oprah had a couple of ex-cons on her show, who had served over ten years each of a **life sentence** for taking the lives of family members. They were both freed because of an amazing technology-DNA Testing. As a result of their tests, it was proven that they were innocent. That in itself is wonderful and not too surprising; what was really surprising was that both men had confessed to the crimes. This left Oprah and the audience amazed. How could this be? Why in the world would anyone do that? Well, the men said that they were traumatized by the situation as well as their **incarceration** and the relentless **interrogation**. This led them to feel confused and battered. At some point they just surrendered and confessed. This made it harder for them to ever be free but at least gave them a temporary peace from all the mental torture. A part of these men was willing to do whatever it took to stop the voices from pounding them relentlessly.

Upon hearing this, I began to weep. I recognized the trauma that most of us have felt in our lives. I remembered the interrogations, the beatings, the verbal abuse etc. and realized that we all had been sold a set of lies. After we had heard them long enough, our psyches started to believe them.

We heard

"Lord, I'm not worthy to receive you."

"What's wrong with you?"

"You should be ashamed of yourself!"

...and the list goes on. This certainly produced **undue hardship** for all of us. Slowly but surely *we began to* ***confess to a crime*** *we didn't do.* We confessed to the crime of "being unlovable," and there would be a horrible **penalty** for believing such a lie.

If you were told anything other than, **"You are a beautiful, perfect, child of God that was born an original blessing!",** then you were lied to. Later, we will learn practices that will deprogram our psyches from believing those lies.

SECTION II

Leniency in the Courtroom

CHAPTER THREE

Five Stages of Forgiveness of Perpetrator and Defendant

"Forgiveness is the fragrance the violet sheds on the heel that has crushed it"
-Mark Twain

Here's how you will know that you have done all your forgiveness work. You won't be here! Forgiveness work is crucial to personal freedom. This is especially true when it comes to self-forgiveness. It's really easy to understand the concept of forgiveness in our minds. We let go of our judgments of ourselves and others and we feel more at peace... Period! Still, that's in the head but not necessarily in our hearts. It can be helpful to hear quips like, ***"not forgiving someone is like taking poison hoping the other person will die."*** That makes it very clear how important for our mental, emotional and even physical health it is to practice forgiveness. True forgiveness encompasses the body and mind. I call this ***Full Body Forgiveness.*** Remember, our Spirit or true nature doesn't need to forgive for it never judged. ***Full Body Forgiveness*** is not a thought but a process.

Here are the 5 stages that I recommend.

1. **Pre-forgiveness.** Before we move into forgiveness, it is important that we deal with our pain in a constructive way. This has been called, *"responding versus reacting."* Our angry emotional/mental state is sometimes referred to as being "pissed off." Imagine that your anger is like urine. It's in there. You can't pretend it away. It needs to be released. It will be very tempting to release that anger onto another. It may also be tempting to take that anger out on oneself, which is tantamount to "pissing against the wind." Neither of these two practices makes life better for you or others. So, we need to find a way to release the anger without it getting onto us or others. Sometimes it is helpful to punch a pillow. Sometimes it can be really powerful to scream, cry or wail. Other times, it is helpful to call someone unrelated to your present hurt and "let it all out." These practices can help us release our anger with-out dumping it onto another or ourselves.

   Imagine that your teenage child backed your new car out of the garage but neglected to open the garage door first. At that moment, you would most likely not feel very calm and forgiving. That is the time to tell that person, "I love you. I know you didn't mean to do it. I need some help right now and when I get it, I will come back and we can talk. Just know that my love for you has not changed one bit." Then you go see a friend that you trust. You may say,-"I want to kill my kid." You just released but not on yourself or your child. A good friend will be able to accept you right where you are and that pure acceptance can help you get calm and centered. In the book, "*Real Love*" by Dr. Greg Baer, this is called "getting filled up." It is very difficult to respond when we are not "filled up." We would most likely react, and that will only feed the imposed guilt in everyone.

2. **I forgive that jerk for what they did to me.** It's very easy to recognize that this stage is not very evolved, but it allows us to feel our pain that is inspiring us to judge ourselves and others. Imagine that someone hits you in the arm. In the immediate moments that follow, it hurts. You are most likely not going to be able to immediately move to ***Full Body Forgiveness***, so stage 2 gives us a starting place. There may be a physical or emotional bruise there, and that bruise may take some time to heal. It is important to be gentle with our physical and emotional selves even though our mental and Spiritual selves may be fully embracing the concept of forgiveness.

3. **I know that they and I did the very best we could within our current state of consciousness.**

"Those who seem to hate you—don't actually hate you at all. They merely despise the change you represent that threatens the foundation of their reality. This is why everyone, including yourself first and foremost, deserves more love, not less."
-Matt Kahn

When Yeshua said *"forgive them, for they know not what they do,"* he wasn't having a very good day. Still, he was fully aware that his persecutors were doing the best they could within their current state of consciousness. This awareness removes all judgment, which is a form of self-inflicted pain. If this is true for others, then it stands to reason that it must also be true for us. We too are doing the best we can within our current state of consciousness. Because this is such an important aspect of our innocence, I will discuss more of this later in **Chapter 6.**

4. **I know that they and I did the ONLY thing we could at the time based on stage 3.** If stage 3 is true, then it also stands to reason that we always did the ONLY thing we could. It is so tempting for us to think, "I should have healed this by now" or "They knew better." These are just our ego's way of not embracing what is and looking for ways to keep us weak and controllable. When we fully melt into the idea that we all did the ONLY thing we could at the time, we are free to grow more fully into our destined experience with joy and acceptance.

5. **I am grateful to them and myself *"for giving"* me this perfect opportunity to grow in this way.**

"Meet your deepest despair with these two words...
Thank you."
-Matt Kahn

Developing an Attitude of Gratitude for your perceived persecutors takes even more consciousness than loving them. Here is an example. Bring to mind a special person that knows where all your buttons are and relishes in pushing them. Do you love them? This is probably so, especially if they are a family member or an old friend. Most of us have spent decades learning to love all the people in our lives on some level. But do you always appreciate them? Probably not, especially when you are triggered as a result of something they said or did. Finding a way to be grateful for each opportunity with a knowing that it would not be happening if there was not something in it for you is a very freeing attitude. At some point, there will be a gift on the other side of the pain. Appreciation is a way of acknowledging the gift. Some will try and move to stage 5 immediately. This usually means that you have forgiven them mentally, but most likely, the heart and body will still be unwilling to go there. The stages gently allow for **Full Body Forgiveness**.

Moving through the 5 stages of forgiveness is best achieved by remaining in one of three states of consciousness.

A. **Pure Acceptance of what is**. You don't have to like it but you will have to at least accept what is. Not accepting what is causes suffering, judgment and prevents us from freedom.

B. **Making the Best of what is**. Once we have fully accepted what is, we can move into seeing the gift that has been presented and use that gift to enhance our lives from this point on.

C. **Making what is, The Best**! This requires us to embrace the **5th Step of Forgiveness** and actually find gratitude for what has occurred while acknowledging that it was the best thing that could have possibly happened for us.

Even the least joyous of these three, **pure acceptance of what is**, still embraces that all is well and couldn't be any different. This is different from **"pseudo-acceptance**" which is, "**the smug idea that others will come around to our way of thinking eventually when the other wakes up to the truth."** Just remember… just because you are working on forgiveness and maybe even reached stage 2 or 3, doesn't mean, as Marianne Williamson says, "**you want to do lunch."**

CHAPTER FOUR

Turning the Other Cheek

"Sometimes the most present thing we can say is a firm NO!
-Eckhart Tolle

We all remember the old way as taught by the Old Testament**, "An eye for an eye and a tooth for a tooth."** Well we all know what that does... it leaves everyone toothless and blind. Then we were told, **"turn the other cheek.**" Well, I always had an issue with that because it felt co-dependent. How many of us have taken what feels like abuse and just stood there allowing for more? Much of this is because we often value what others think of us more than we value ourselves.

In 2008, I began to reconnect with my surrogate mother whom I had been estranged from for 12 years. I was so excited, and I rejoiced in another opportunity to heal old wounds and start over from a new, more awakened place. By 2010, we were talking almost every day, and our relationship had truly become closer than ever. One day, she left me a particularly disturbing message, and it really crushed me. I decided that if I were to continue to stay connected with her, then it was important that I let her know how her message landed on me and request that she not say things like that to me anymore. Angelina lovingly reminded me that the last time I had questioned my surrogate mother about something she said and told her how it landed on me; she stopped talking to me for 12 years. The question now came down to, "Are you willing to jeopardize your connection with her in order to stay true to your heart and make an authentic, caring request?" I merely said to Angelina, ***"Yes, because finally, I love myself more than I love her loving me."***

When I did the 12-steps in CoDA (Codependents Anonymous), I learned a lot about what enabling was. I realize that often, people are driven to act out in certain ways. When we do nothing or encourage it, we are feeding their **wounded prisoner** and bringing in more abuse. **When you stand up to any bully, whether internal or external, by embracing the words, "***I love myself, more than I love you loving me,***" you are acting in the opposite of codependence. You are building a foundation of self-love that actually strengthens your ability to love everyone and everything else in a more profound way. **Play track 1-I Love Myself**

I Love Myself

By Armand Della Volpe

I love myself, more than I love you loving me,
I love myself my love.

Are there people in your life who **don't get you** who **you don't get** either, but you want to feel peaceful about them? Welcome to one of the most challenging postures in **relationship yoga**. I call these, "**creditor relationships.**" How about treating them like a "creditor?" They don't consciously have your best interest at heart, and they want something from you that you aren't willing to give them. Love them from afar. Don't give them any information or warmth that they'll use to try and collect more from you. They are not wrong for trying to get what they believe you owe them. You are not wrong for not believing you owe them. It's just a stalemate. In *Eckankar,*— they describe it this way…"**Give either warm love or charity. One gives warm love to those who give it back, charity to all else; love with no expectations/ no contracts."** As a person who has spent the better part of his life trying to give warm love to everybody, I can say clearly that it has been the source of much of my suffering. We can be honest, direct and clear when we deal with "**creditor relationships,**" Often, the less contact the better. It's important to remember that **it is never healthy or freeing to close our hearts to anyone or anything.** Creating healthy boundaries however, benefits everyone.

In 2012, after experiencing about 24 months of relationship heaven with my surrogate mother, our old "**creditor relationship"** began to surface again. We tried hard to come to a meeting of the minds but alas, like oil and water, our energetic polarities just separated again.

We ended up simply agreeing to disagree and went our separate ways six months later. It was painful, but this separation didn't have the drama of the past. This was more of a joint agreement where each realized that we could better love each other from afar.

This brings us back to Jesus' quote. I have my own translation of *"turn the other cheek."* What if he was misquoted? What if the translation from Aramaic to English was flawed? What if Jesus and other great prophets were not telling us to just take it? What if the actual quote was, *"Turn the other cheeks and walk away."*? Doesn't that make more sense? Then, we can lovingly turn the other cheeks and move in a different direction.

The biggest lesson I learned from our dog Boomerang (that we co-own with our dear friend Jodi Floyd) was, *"If you are kicked by someone, don't go back and bite them. Instead, go find someone who will love you, pet you, hold you, tend to your wounds, and keep you safe."* Thanks to all of you that tended to me this week. Thanks also to those who I perceived to have kicked me. All have equally raised me up. **Play track 2-I Forgive You**

I Forgive You

By Armand Della Volpe and Fred Bogert

Haunted by the times you made me cry,
Feeling not quite good enough not understanding why,
I blamed you for the hell that I was in,
Then I burned through my resentment, so I could love again.

I forgive you, for you know not what you do,
When you did those things, that hurt so much,
you didn't have a clue.
Love needs no conditions; it will always see us through,
I forgive you… for you know not what you do.

I still have an angry thought or two,
I don't do well with those that try and tell me what to do,
But I still try and turn the other cheek,
Watch me walk away you'll know exactly what I mean.

I forgive you, for you know not what you do,
When you do those things, that hurt so much,
you haven't got a clue.
Love needs no conditions; it will always see us through,
I forgive you… for you know not what you do.

The more you give away, the more you have,
Everyone's a mirror of some part of you,
It could be anger, or it could be love.

Haunted by the times I made you cry,
I showed you the worst in me, not understanding why,
But we can heal together perfectly,
I can be more loving but there's one thing that I need…

Please forgive me, for I know not what I do,
When I do those things that hurt so much,
I haven't got a clue,
Love needs no conditions; it will always see us through,
Please forgive me… For I know not what I do.
Please forgive me…. I forgive you.

CHAPTER FIVE

Pleading for God's Mercy

Asking God for forgiveness is about as outlandish as asking the moon to apologize for an eclipse. Desiring forgiveness from The Universe is only appealing because our imprisoned minds have imagined separation, leading to judgment, etc. When we can embrace our **true nature** of innate perfection and see this world for the "dream" that it truly is; we can let go of the notion that any part of us needs to be different than it is. Then we will embrace complete forgiveness within ourselves and paradoxically recognize there was nothing to forgive. Go figure! Still, forgiveness and apologies continue to be an important healing and resolution tool on Earth, which I like to call "*Planet Disney*." I highly recommend them and use them often with wonderful effective results.

SECTION III

Calling the Defense to the Stand

CHAPTER SIX

My Client Did the Very Best They Could

"God said love your enemy
and I obeyed and loved myself"
-Kahlil Gibran

We have all heard, "Do the best you can" or "Always do your best." Something always felt funny to me about this, but still, I adhered to it. This was a great way to feel guilty if we imagine that we didn't do our best. As recognized in the 5 Stages of Forgiveness in **Chapter 3**, we always do the best we can within our current state of consciousness. That doesn't mean we can't do better at some other time; it just means we don't need to feel bad about ourselves relative to anything we've done.

But what if you grow in consciousness and realize that you treated someone in a way that from your new perspective, you would have done differently? Great! That means you have grown, not that you did anything wrong. **Making amends should be a joyous, heavenly adventure into personal evolution**. Instead, it is often a tedious, self-deprecating, guilt-ridden hell. I personally have struggled with this my whole life. I have been the *King of Amends.* This was disguised as an altruistic move. I eventually realized that beneath the altruism was a self-loathing designed to keep me always feeling like I could have done better, and I had better be punished for it. My beloved bride, Angelina, calls this, "Schindler's Dilemma." "***Schindler's List*** is a 1993 American epic historical period drama film directed and co-produced by Steven Spielberg. The film relates a period in the life of Oskar Schindler, an ethnic German businessman, during which he saved the lives of more than a thousand mostly Polish-Jewish refugees from the Holocaust by employing them in his factories." No matter how much Schindler did and how many lives he saved, he always felt he could have done more. It is time to pardon the "Schindler" in all of us and give ourselves the credit we deserve.

Most of us find it easier to let others off the hook while realizing that they did the best they could, but we are much more reluctant to offer ourselves the same leniency. Recognizing that we always do the best we can, allows us to feel innocent and lovable regardless of how we show up in any given instance. That self-love will give us the foundation to joyously grow, admit when we were unskillful, make amends if appropriate, and all the while feel perfectly **innocent** through each stage of our evolution.

CHAPTER SEVEN

False Evidence by the Prosecution

"Illusion is viewing yourself less desirably than the Universe does."
-Matt Kahn

One of our biggest fears is, "What if I get it wrong?" You have probably heard that **F.E.A.R.** can stand for **F**alse **E**vidence **A**ppearing **R**eal. Unless of course you are being chased by a wild animal, in which case, it stands for **Forget Everything And Run**. My favorite is **Feel Everything And Release**. The fear is coming up for a reason, and there is a gift if we are open to receiving it.

So, what do we do about our fear of not doing things right? Again, we are always doing the best we can at any given moment. So is everyone else. That would imply that *We Can't Get It Wrong*. Fully embracing the concept that *We Can't Get It Wrong* will replace any old fear of not doing things right. Even simple physics states, "*Two objects cannot occupy the same space at the same time.*" This also holds true of states of consciousness. We cannot have a deep belief that *We Can't Get It Wrong* and still be afraid of not doing things right. Unfortunately, most of us have had decades of entertaining the fear of not doing things right; so, it will take some time and effort to remove those old false viruses by feeding ourselves enough healing truth. Remember, your psyche is like your computer, in that it doesn't discern whether something is true or not, it only responds to what was programmed into it.

So, if what was programmed into our psyche does not give us peace, why would we believe it? Here are two reasons:

1. It is because we were told that things that happened to us in our childhood were "bad," and the people who did them were "bad."

2. It is because we have been convinced that our mind always knows what's best for us.

Our soul does not know the difference between ourselves, events and others, so the minute we say something or someone else is "bad," a part of us feels "bad." In the movie, "*A Beautiful Life*," the little boy pretended/made-up, with the coaching of his dad, that everything was just a game. As a result, he had a good time even though there was apparent insanity all around him. I invite us all to be more like him. Some may say, "That's not realistic." I would agree, but would you rather be realistic and miserable or idealistic and happy?

So why would you spend so much time believing thoughts that feel bad? It is because those thoughts feed our "*wounded prisoners.*" If our "*wounded prisoner*" is hungry, then it will inspire us to make up and/or believe something that feels bad. Remember the story about the two wolves? Here is how the story goes:

An old Cherokee is teaching his grandson about life. "A fight is going on inside me," he said to the boy.

"It is a terrible fight and it is between two wolves. One is evil – he is anger, envy, sorrow, regret, greed, arrogance, self-pity, guilt, resentment, inferiority, lies, false pride, superiority, and ego." He continued, "The other is good – he is joy, peace, love, hope, serenity, humility, kindness, benevolence, empathy, generosity, truth, compassion, and faith. The same fight is going on inside you – and inside every other person, too."

The grandson thought about it for a minute and then asked his grandfather, "Which wolf will win?"

The old Cherokee simply replied, "The one you feed."

The more I make up and believe, aka "make-believe," that this world is a wonderful, safe, magical playground, the more joy I feel and the more fun I have. The more I see all people as playing out their roles perfectly, whether pleasant or not, the more peace I feel. The more I act as if I cannot fail, the more free I feel. The more I surrender to the perfection of everything, the more faith I feel. The more appreciation I have for the people in my life, the more love I feel. The more I see myself as equally wonderful as anyone else, the more *in-love* I feel.

CHAPTER EIGHT

You Get an A+ With Extra Credit

Do you ever look at a sapling and say, "Wow, you could be so much more."? Do you ever look at a dying tree and say, "Sorry, you did it wrong."? Of course not, because we know that throughout all of nature, every life-form is perfect and expressing its perfection through whatever stages it is going through. If God were a teacher handing out grades, a sapling would get an A+ with extra credit for being a perfect sapling. A small tree would get the same, as a tall tree… An A+ with extra credit. A dying tree would get an A+ with extra credit for dying so perfectly. Why not the same for us? Are you aware that no one who has ever lived or will ever live can play your song as well as you? That makes you the ultimate YOU in the Universe. Of course, it's also true of everyone else.

When I teach my Native American flute classes, I always give everyone who takes the class an A+ with extra credit. I do this because I know that they are the best in the world at playing their song, and I grade them accordingly. I imagine us all in a variety of life-lesson grades. Some are in preschool, some in kindergarten, some in elementary, etc. etc. Preschool is not less worthy, beautiful or perfect than post graduate studies. We may have a PhD in one area and be in preschool in another. So what? We are exactly where we are until we are somewhere else. We can even go back and repeat a grade if we choose or if our soul wants more clarity in that area. It is of great benefit for us to start loving and accepting ourselves fully right where we are as well as doing the same for everyone and everything else. We can give A+'s with extra credit to everyone and everything for their perfection. This is not an academic or skill grade which is used for performance, skill or completion of a required course of study but a grade for the perfection of each person's humanity.

The next time someone shows up in your life and annoys the heck out of you, give them an A+ with extra credit for doing such a fabulous job of annoying you. Allow that annoyance to open your heart more. Recognize that they are exactly where they are supposed to be. Allow the annoyance to be a light shining on an old wound under the surface that is now exposed. Imagine there to be a splinter in that wound. As long as no one touches the area, you may not even know it's there. Let your acceptance and awareness become the tweezers that pull that splinter out. Eventually, you can move to Stage 5 of forgiveness and actually thank your teacher for helping you get that darn splinter out.

Armand "AJ" age: 7

SECTION IV

Holding Nothing Back From Your Testimony

CHAPTER NINE

Telling the Whole Nekkid Truth

"I much prefer to look weak and feel strong than to look strong and feel weak."
-Goofball Guru

"Kites rise highest against the wind - not with it."
-Winston Churchill

You may have heard the saying, "We have to feel it to heal it." The more we resist our feelings, the more we suffer. Pain is inevitable, but prolonged suffering is optional. We invite prolonged suffering when we say, "This tragedy shouldn't have happened." or "I can't allow myself to feel this." Paulo Coelho wrote, *"Tell your heart that the fear of suffering is worse than the suffering itself. And no heart has ever suffered when it goes in search of its dream."* I would add to that **"as long as we are not attached to the dream's fulfillment."**

The Abraham Hicks material calls feelings our *emotional guidance system.* I like to think of it as our body's GPS that is doing everything possible to keep us on the most joyous, peaceful path. When we have a feeling that is painful, our GPS is saying "redirecting route." In order to get on the best route, we must allow ourselves to feel those feelings and allow them to guide us. Otherwise, we will resist and fight to stay on the path we are on.

In September of 2011, for the first time in my life, I decided to empty myself of anything I could that was numbing me from feeling what was really going on inside me. I stopped booking almost any work since I realized that I got lots of attention and approval from my appearances. I gave up any fantasies about women or career. I entered three long-term recovery support groups to keep me sober from anything that might distract me. I challenged all my *Spiritual* beliefs about positivity, law of attraction, free will, etc. to make sure I wasn't using God/Spirituality to avoid my pain. I started studying *"Real Love"*** by Greg Baer and attending ***"Real Love Groups"*** as often as I could. I even tried periods of celibacy to keep me from, "using Angelina as a drug." I will speak more about this later in **Chapter 32,** but just know that my decision to allow myself to feel what I was most afraid of, rather than stay in my comfort zone turned out to be one of the most freeing decisions of my life.

You too may be stuck on a path that feels safer to you but doesn't truly bring you peace and freedom. Michael Singer in *The Untethered Soul* compares this path of safety to an invisible fence, similar to what many create for their dogs and cats. Whenever the animal gets near the fence, there is a mild electric shock that is felt through some sort of collar. The older we get, the more of these invisible fences we tend to create. We think they are keeping us safe, but in actuality, they are keeping us from feeling free and truly at peace. Only by being willing to face the pain of moving through our feelings, can we actually realize that the invisible fence was only an illusion, and the pain is only temporary.

What if your dog were reading this book? **Stop now and enter that dog on *America's Got Talent!*** Anyway, your dog decides that they are willing to feel the pain of the electric fence in order to potentially have more peace and freedom. As they approach the fence, they feel the shock. They move closer and the shock is greater. If they continue to allow themselves to feel the pain while moving closer and closer to the fence, then eventually they will move completely through the invisible electric fence and get past the pain and limitations. Imagine how free and happy they will feel as they now have a whole new world to explore. We all have this same opportunity. We can move toward the things that cause us pain and move through the pain to freedom. This will require surrender and trust. Once we own our feelings about the past, we can release them and replace them with new feelings that arise from knowing our life was/is perfect just the way it was/is. **Play track 3-Learning How to Feel**

Learning How to Feel

By Armand Della Volpe

There was a home, there was a family, there was a child-hood,
Didn't know what was going on, didn't know what was going on,
Everything safe, everything warm, everything stable,
Fell apart before my eyes and started feeling wrong,
So I found myself a story that would justify my hurt,
Talked myself into believing, I could hide behind my words.

So I learned how to think, I learned how to do,
I sought my completion; I thought it was you,
I need to surrender, so I can know what's real,
I'm going back to a world of innocence, learning how to feel.

Scared of my anger, running from lonely, didn't do sadness,
Just put on a happy face, just put on a happy face,
Constantly searching for a new romance, some stimulation,
Never really satisfied what I was hungry for,
Found myself with lots of women telling me I was OK,
Always seeking validation, but it always went away.
'Cause I learned how to think, I learned how to do,
I sought my completion; I thought it was you,

I need to surrender, so I can know what's real,
I'm going back to a world of innocence…

Where is my joy? The drug's no longer working,
I'm so bored with all that used to make me feel alive,
I'm a scared angry boy, who wants to punish someone,
I'm so sorry if I took it out on you, now I'm learning how to feel.

Where is my joy? The drug's no longer working,
I'm so bored with all that used to make me feel alive,
I'm a sad angry boy, who wants to punish someone,
I'm so sorry if I took it out, so sorry if I take it out on you,

Now I'm learning how to feel, less concerned with what to do,
I 'm finding my completion and I'm sharing it with you,
Learning how to surrender, so I can know what's real,
I'm going back to a world of innocence, learning how to feel.
Learning how to feel, and it's helping me to heal,
Now that I'm learning how to feel,
and it's getting pretty real,
Now that I'm learning how to feel… Learning how to feel.

CHAPTER TEN

If I Start Crying on the Stand, I May Never Stop

"Out of suffering have emerged the strongest souls; the most massive characters are seared with scars."
- Khalil Gibran

I have had several men tell me over the years that they wouldn't allow themselves to cry anymore. The most common reason they gave was that ***they were afraid that if they started, they might never stop***. This broke my heart. I know that allowing ourselves to cry is one of the most healing things we can do. Still, I understand why someone would not want to surrender that much.

I am going to use a word here than may trigger some. I invite you to reserve judgment and just hear me out because there is great power and freedom in what I am about to tell you. I believe that we are all born with a "bipolar heart." What I mean by this is that we are meant to experience the full spectrum of emotions and feelings. The trick is to keep the prison gates to our heart open enough that the emotions can be felt and then released. That way, we get to experience all that Life has to offer while bringing ourselves back to a state of equilibrium and peace.

As a HUGE roller coaster fanatic, I love when Life takes me on *an emotional and/or mental roller coaster.* Imagine that Life is just an elaborate thrill ride. No matter how intense the ride is or how scary the thrills are, most of us don't get off a roller coaster and spend the rest of our lives suffering over the experience. That is because we know that it was just a ride. If it really messed with us, it may stick with us a bit longer… but still, we recognize that all the perceived danger was just an illusion designed to literally, *"scare/thrill the hell out of us."* That is because we allowed ourselves to experience the ride, but when we got off the ride, we could get back to reality. We can do this with Life and the full range of emotions that we experience. We just don't want to ever get stuck on the ride, and that actually happened to me once at King's Island Theme Park in Cincinnati. We were just about to take off and the seat completely reclined to a lying position. I had never lain down completely on a roller coaster before, so I was quite excited. The ride's safety system shut it all down, and it took about 30 minutes to address the situation, bypass the safety system, and reset. I was already doing daily meditation, so I just closed my eyes and started to meditate. It was actually a very relaxing time. **The trick is not to get stuck in Life!**

CHAPTER ELEVEN

And Nothing But the Truth ...aka Pigs Can't Sing

"Never attempt to teach a pig to sing; it wastes your time and annoys the pig."
- Robert A. Heinlein

We've all heard the biggest lies right:

"The check is in the mail."

"I'll still respect you in the morning."

"I've never done this before" Etc.

Well, I uncovered another one... *"If I give them enough love, they'll love me back."* I believe that recognizing this lie would save us all a lot of trouble and disappointment!

In December of 2011, I was attending a *Real Love* meeting in Phoenix, AZ when I shared that I was in an uncomfortable relationship off and on for eight years with a former musical partner of mine and his wife. The facilitator said, "You are uncomfortable with your relationship because you are not able to give love to them." I was like, "No way. I have been trying to give them love for eight years, and they resent me and write and say mean things to and about me." I felt very righteous in my stance of giving love regardless of how I was treated. The next words shook me in my shoes, and I would never be the same again. The facilitator asked, **"Have you fully accepted them, even when they resent you and say mean things to and about you?"** Oh shit! I had to admit that I was trying to change them. I wasn't fully accepting of them right where they were, which is what every human craves. My love was very conditional, which meant it wasn't love at all. Once I got this, I was able to love, accept and allow them to be exactly who they were. I was spending tons of energy on trying to figure out what I could say and do to get them to be more loving towards me. Better to spend our energy on those who can receive it. Some people just are unable to love us the way we want to be loved... no need to make them wrong. We just get to be realistic and let go of all expectations that they will be any different. We can love them right where they are since to do otherwise is painful.

And, when we generously give love with no expectations or even the desire to have our generosity returned, we tap into the "Law of Attraction" without attachment or potential disappointment. As Matt Kahn so beautifully says *"Despite how open, peaceful, and loving you attempt to be, people can only meet you, as deeply as they've met themselves. This is the heart of clarity."*

CHAPTER TWELVE

When You Just Can't Seem to Stop Fighting With Other Inmates

Of course, each of us has wounded parts. I call them *wounded prisoners,* for they are stuck in the pain of the past. Have you ever known someone with whom you absolutely felt a strong connection, yet if you spent too much time or had too much intimate communication with them, there was volatile conflict? As said in **Chapter Four**, these relationships are so challenging because in a **"creditor relationship,"** each *wounded prisoner* is more likely to trigger the other. With these folks, casual relationship may work but not much more. But what if you **don't** want to just be casual friends with someone with whom you have this **triggering wounded prisoner** dynamic? This will require much finesse, self-care, courage and compassion. To my knowledge, there has only been one person in my life with whom I share a **"triggering wounded prisoner"** dynamic where we have been able to move past the pain into deep, connected, healthy relationship.

Volatile conflict is often the result when **triggering wounded prisoners spend too much time together**. Imagine that these **wounded prisoners** are like *guard dogs.* You and your friend absolutely adore each other, and you each have at least one of these *guard dogs* with you at all times. Sometimes the *dog* is locked up. Sometimes it is free to roam, and other times it is on a leash. The trick is to make sure these *guard dogs* don't get too close to each other because there will be a fight and most likely some emotional, mental or even physical bloodshed. If either party had a healed **prisoner,** then the other *dog* would have nothing with which to fight. Some people's *guard dog* is free to roam, is unrecognized, and will bark and bite anyone at any time. Unfortunately, unless our wounded prisoners are fully healed**,** other people's *dogs* are gonna find ours and pick a fight. For most of us, our *guard dogs* are either locked away/unrecognized or leashed/recognized. As long as everyone involved in a triggering wounded prisoner dynamic has recognized their **guard dogs** and are conscious of how to keep them on a short leash while healing them, they will be able to have intimate conscious loving relationship.

As I said, this is serious relationship yoga and I am only just beginning to learn to navigate these waters. Fortunately, in my relationship with Angelina, our *wounded prisoners* rarely fight with each other. This is what I call **complementary wounded prisoners.** Most of my friends are complementary with me and I have often *avoided or run away* from those people who were too triggering. I realize that I did this to protect myself, which in many cases prevented me from becoming more conscious and healed. I now choose to practice personal **guard dog taming** when I encounter those with **triggering wound-**

ed prisoners. This keeps me very aware of the dynamic without a need to abandon others or judge them for my pain. As always, we can eventually become thankful to all our triggers, as they continue to inspire us to heal and fully embrace our own *guard dogs.*

SECTION V

We Are Victims of Identity Theft

CHAPTER THIRTEEN

Who's that Cellmate in My Head?

"Thoughts are not powerful in and of themselves. They only become powerful when we believe them."
-Adyashanti

Our body and mind were given to us as tools to assist us in this physical life. Unfortunately, the ego mind decided to take over. It is an imposter that is posing as us and pretending to be us. Eckhart Tolle refers to this as "*the phantom self.*" You see that picture on your driver's license? That is not really you. It is just the face of a temporary body that you inhabit. The imposter wants you to believe that it is you so it can control you and protect you. This imposter does not operate in your best interest. It operates in what it thinks is in your best interest. It is not objective and only regurgitates what you and everyone else have dumped into it. It is no more objectively helpful to you than any other computer.

Actually, most of the time, your mind is saying negative things about you since most of what has been downloaded is negative. Like a TV broadcast, it is constantly transmitting and constantly receiving. It is no more you than your TV. You can turn it down. You can watch it. You can even believe it, but that doesn't make it any more real. You have a TV and you have a mind, but neither of them are you. Your mind can be useful; yet most of it will not evolve you or bring you any peace or happiness. This cellmate is obnoxious, and must be tamed if we are going to find real peace.

I have found meditation to be the best way to quiet the cellmate. Still, he will try and distract me any time I begin to blow his cover.

One day, I was about to do my morning meditation practice. About three minutes in, I started to slip into a blissful place. I heard my cellmate say, "What a useless waste of time."

I didn't respond in thought but went back to focusing on quieting the mind. Then my cellmate said, "Don't you have some gigs to book? I know you have some churches to call."

I started engaging him and even spoke back to him in my mind. I told him that meditation was the most important thing I could do and that all my other tasks would happen more efficiently and joyously if I gave myself some quiet time each morning and night. I realized I was conversing with a neurotic lunatic.

Again, I had been pulled from my quiet space by the imposter. I managed to remind my cellmate that I no longer believed him, but it was too late, I was distracted. I went to Angelina, told her the story and wrote this song.

Play track 4-Voices In My Head

Voices In My Head

By Armand Della Volpe

I hear the voices in my head but I'm not listening,
They try and tell me that I'm not okay,
I hear the voices in my head but I'm not listening,
The silence offers me another way.

In the space behind the voices, pure awareness comforts me,
In the space behind the voices, I am love and I am free.

CHAPTER FOURTEEN

When the Prosecution Says You Have More Work to Do

Sometimes we may find ourselves wanting to get away from our house and/or work. This happens quite often for me, and it's one of the things that motivates me to do *outdoor exercise, take yoga classes and play tennis.* Sometimes, our homes and/or workplaces represent all the things that we have to do, and the story we've made up about how far behind we are in getting them done. My *Guru Voice* will remind me from time to time, **"You Never Get It All Done,"** or what Garth said in *Wayne's World,* "**Live in the Now, Wayne.**" Each time I hear it, I feel **more at ease**. These types of phrases can help us realize that we are the ones who put the deadlines for our achievements upon us. The Universe has no such criteria. So what if we don't get everything done in the time frame we set forth! Life is messy sometimes. We always get everything done that we need to do. **"It's more important to FEEL and BE than it is to DO."**

When we can **let go of the rigid demands we put upon ourselves** about time frames, etc., we will start to see all the projects, organizing, work materials, etc. as ***"works in progress"*** that are an indication that we are evolving and active. Then we will feel less eager to get away from our homes and/or work. We can still plan to do things outside of work and/or home, but we will be going towards them instead of away from our perceived burdens of responsibility.

CHAPTER FIFTEEN

Beware When the Warden Says, "I'm Proud of You."

It occurred to me that being proud of ourselves, our kids, our parents, our countries, our race, our religion, our sports teams, our partners, etc., can be a trap. People say it all the time. "I'm so proud of myself" or "I'm so proud of my kid." Someone was recently telling us how **proud** they were of us and our career. I felt my stomach get tight. I didn't say anything to them because I knew they meant it as a compliment. Actually, it usually is said as a compliment and to validate someone, so ultimately I have no issue with it. When I had some time to ponder it, I realized that the phrase **"proud of"** usually means **"pleased with,"** but that seemingly harmless phrase has a very ugly lover/bedfellow. Its name is **"ashamed of,"** and it may accompany its lover just waiting for the opportunity to turn the table.

Sometimes, it can feel a bit condescending when someone says, "I'm proud of you," as if they are giving you their seal of approval, as if you need that approval in order to be OK. ***Beware my friend...*** all that glorious approval will often turn into disapproval. The "*prosecution sea monkeys*" will get their life-giving **fix**, and you will start to feel **unlovable** again.

Like any other addiction… and yes, I use the word addiction when dealing with "**getting the approval**" of others…, there is a really negative side-effect. You begin to crave or need the drug again and again. Wouldn't it be nice if there was a way to indulge in our "**drugs of choice**" and not have any of the side-effects? I, like most folks recovering from addictions, have tried every possible way to be the first person to do this. It's very much like "attachment." You can't have it by itself. Oh no… it always comes with a big dose of suffering. **Pride and Shame** are flip sides of the same coin, and when I consciously let go of shame… pride left too. I miss pride sometimes, but I don't miss shame. The same is true of superiority/inferiority, respect/disrespect, etc. In the words of Forrest Gump, "*They go together like peas and carrots.*"

So, the next time you find yourself feeling **"proud of"** yourself or anyone else, check in and see what you are feeling deeply. It's most likely admiration, joy, warmth, open-heartedness or peace. Make sure it's not laced with judgment that will turn to shame when you don't feel the same way. Let yourself or the other know that you are feeling more connected to them, more peaceful or more open-hearted. This keeps it about you and will not as likely feed the ego's desire for approval. Oh, and don't go trying to kill the "*prosecution sea monkeys.*" They are relatively harmless unless snorted into your consciousness and then they can mess you up when they come to life in your nasal passages. I'm just sayin'...

CHAPTER SIXTEEN

Giving Ourselves the Death Penalty

Feeling unworthy to be alive, compounded by the voices in our heads that often overwhelm us with worst case scenarios, constant interrogation and prosecution can easily convince us that life is not really worth living. Suicide (Robin Williams comes painfully to mind) is the most obvious example of this death wish, but this can show up in many more subtle ways and can be very unconscious. Choosing to not take care of our bodies can be a form of suicide.

With rare exception, everyone is aware that a certain amount of exercise and a healthy diet will enhance the body and make the human experience more enjoyable and lasting. Diet is probably the most subjective of topics, but still, most of us have at least an idea of which food is health enhancing and which food is not. Most would agree that fresh fruits and vegetables are healthy for our bodies and that fried butter sticks, cookies, candies and sodas are not. Still, because we don't feel worthy of life, there will be an unconscious resistance to doing what may enhance our health and longevity. We also seek out comfort foods and other dopamine producing substances and behaviors that compensate for our lack of joy and the biological chemicals that are produced with joy. Chapter 26 will address ways to get the natural highs that we are all craving.

Here is one way I chose to give myself the death penalty. Decades of inflammatory thoughts and emotions as a result of my previous programming led to some artery damage in the left anterior descending artery in my heart. In order to fix the problem, my body sent cholesterol to naturally repair the damage. This is a wonderful way that the body tries to keep us healthy. Unfortunately, if we keep damaging the artery, the cholesterol will layer up more and more to patch us up, eventually restricting the flow of blood. If the artery gets small enough, like mine did at a 55% blockage, a hemorrhage of some of the plaque, which can be caused by stress (inflammation), overheating or over-exertion, can clog the artery so much that the result is.......... wait for it.........

HEART ATTACK

This is also known as "The Widow Maker" because typically, the first symptom of this condition is death. Fortunately, I only released enough plaque to cause severe chest pains, which led me to a full diagnosis so I could take appropriate action. I used a low inflammation diet, along with extra exercise, natural and prescription supplements to keep the cholesterol manageable while I fixed the problem and most importantly, began reducing my emotional stress through meditation and practicing the principles I am sharing in this book.

I had gotten a clear message from The Universe. "It is time to make a deeper commitment to reducing inflammation in your life. This means letting go of **inflammatory relationships** as well. You know which relationships add peace and support in your life, but you somehow feel that it is your job to subject yourself to inflammatory relationships in order to prove to yourself that you can rise above the pain and negativity. While those are worthwhile causes, your sensitive heart pays the price. If you want to live a long, healthy, peaceful life, you had better lighten up on yourself, and be kinder to your sensitive inner child and heart, and dramatically limit your time with those that purposely test you."

I knew it was time to commit more fully to my sweet sensitive inner child and heart, while letting go of "my incessant need to subject myself to stormy relationships" in order to improve my navigational skills. Life began to improve dramatically in the peace, joy and self-love department. I felt like I had added more glitter to my world, and who doesn't love glitter?

CHAPTER SEVENTEEN

To Meditate or Medicate, That Is the Question

"More than ever, we will be wise to stay in the observer mode rather than get caught up in all the drama. Biblically speaking, 'be in the world not of the world.'"
-Goofball Guru

The more I explored emotions, addictions and physical sensation, the more I recognized that we are all just seeking ways to "feel good" and quiet those voices in our heads. Unfortunately, in our pursuit of pleasure and avoidance of pain, we can just as easily get hooked on negative emotions (chemicals) as positive ones. As the movie, "***What the Bleep Do We Know?***" so clearly showed, *"We are all chemical producing machines. Our cells get addicted to certain chemicals, and we get our organs to produce more and more so we can continue to get the* ***rush.****"*

I have almost always avoided drugs. I avoided illegal drugs for the obvious reasons and pharmaceuticals for my stance that, *"They only offered symptomatic relief and were addictive with horrible side-effects."* I actually was quite righteous about this since I thought that *drug users of any kind were just not courageous enough to heal the problem at its core.* That was obviously just a way to judge that behavior so I could feel superior rather than explore what was really compelling those to pursue relief.

I spent most of 2012 doing a lot of research into addictions and I realized that all of them seem to be producing the same thing... **Drugs**! This drug is most often some form of Dopamine, but ultimately it produces a HIGH. All these years of righteousness, I was just substituting the Dope of substances for the Dope of… Romance, Sex, Praise, Fantasy, Rejection, Fear, Martyrdom and Compulsive Thinking *(which is usually just a way to avoid **The Now** and ponder our own separation and not-enough-ness).*

Dopamine is produced by so many of the things we get addicted and attached to: **Shopping, Gambling, Intense Movies, Eating, Sugar, Coffee, Energy Drinks, Chocolate, Alcohol, Drugs, Performing, Working, Making Money, Spending Money, Fantasy** (which includes sex, lifestyle, finances, justice, peace on earth, etc.). Even things that might appear to be painful like self-sacrifice, being a victim and complaining, can often trigger a sense of pride and/or pity that has its own Dopamine-like chemical payoff. In other words…, **we are all just medicating.**

For 16 months, I experimented with Deep Meditation for approximately two hours per day. I even explored a few "entheogens" to see what all the hype was about. My new take on all of these drugs is... **Meditate or Medicate!** Meditation seems to produce its own **"feel good"** chemical often referred to as DMT. This comes from our own pineal gland and produces an altered state where we **recognize that we are... perfect, all-loving children of the universe, connected to all other matter. It also may heighten awareness about unresolved issues.** My favorite benefit from meditation is that the "voices in my head" get very quiet, and the voice of my soul gets amplified. Isn't that what happens when we commit deeply to a spiritual path or spiritual course of study? ***Isn't that the absolute reality anyway and not the one our egos have imagined?***

What if cravings were merely our guidance letting us know that we need more stillness and contemplative time to remember who we really are and quiet the neurotic voices in our heads? What if we are using the "satisfaction of distraction" as a way to numb out the pain of believing a lie that we are small and separate? I'm not criticizing drugs of any type. I now believe that anything can be used to raise our consciousness or to medicate and numb out. The more I learn about alcohol, refined sugar and pharmaceutical drugs, *especially those used for mental and emotional conditions,* the more I am amazed that they are so available and legal, when many things with a fraction of the side-effects and negative repercussions are illegal and demonized.

At times, the imposter convinces me that I can relax my meditation, spiritual intake and exercise practices a bit. As a result, I slip back into listening to the voices in my head and becoming less of an observer. Fortunately, that is painful enough to get me back on track. It feels a bit like getting one's teeth cleaned professionally and thinking, "Now I don't have to brush and floss daily." The crud just comes back. So, my question to all of us is... **Medicate or Meditate**?

SECTION VI

Viewing All the Evidence

CHAPTER EIGHTEEN

Calling In the Impeccable Witness

"The most important and valuable thing we have to do is this... stay present to who we are. This sounds simple but is not so easy. We are not our personalities, our bodies, our jobs or our relationships. We are simply eternal, divine beings. Seek ye first the kingdom. In other words, see and know yourself as a God spark and all else will beautifully fall into place."
-Goofball Guru

We are so worthy to receive all the love in the world. We have nothing to be ashamed of and have no need to ever feel guilty. As Marianne Williamson said, "It is our greatness that we most fear..." Why? Because it is so contradictory to what we've been told. We are so afraid of being arrogant that we play unhealthily small. Arrogance is, "I'm wonderful and Godly, and you're not." Enlightenment is, "I'm wonderful, Godly and totally unique...just like everyone else." (As paraphrased from Swami Beyondananda)- If you are like me, you are in the process of rediscovering your **innocence,** your divinity and your ultimate worthiness. We have been serving time for a crime we didn't commit. This has gone on too long.

As we move into what Eckhart Tolle referred to as *The New Earth,* humanity is being reminded of Yeshua's amazing words**,** "Love thy neighbor **as thyself.**" Somehow, we often forget the **'as thyself'** part. For most of us, it's much easier to love God and our neighbor than it is to love ourselves. **This has got to stop**. We are of the most good to others and the planet when we are free. How can we be free if we are imprisoned in our mind from an old sentence that we never deserved?

CHAPTER NINETEEN

Loving the Convict the Way God Does

"Admiration is how the Divine recognizes itself in another"
-Matt Kahn

Self-Love has been a quest for me for over 20 years with intermittent success. I have noticed this... *when I am feeling and expressing love for myself, I feel really safe and happy. When I don't, I feel scared and sad.*

Once during a meditation, I felt an overwhelming sense of **self-love**. I decided to slip out of meditation to ponder what was going on. What came to me was this... ***In order for me to fully love myself, there must be space between Lover and Loved.***

When I observe a child, nature and/or the beauty of anyone, I can easily recognize the divinity and lovability of that which I am observing. The challenge with loving ourselves is that we often don't create the space between the "**I**" that is doing the loving and recognizing the beauty, and the "**myself**" which is being showered with the love.

Meditation always takes me into observer mode. The challenge is *how to bring that state of consciousness into the*

Matrix and my human world. Most of my Spiritual Teachers have promoted the importance of becoming the ***"witness," "observer,"*** etc. Whenever we get absorbed into our human drama, it is important to create some space so we can more fully love and guide our human from a clearer place.

During the first three years of my relationship with Angelina, it seemed really easy to feel lovable and to love myself the way the Universe does. Of course I was completely inebriated with "*love drugs.*" My romance with Angelina was so intense and affirming that my cellmate was not able to get to me. Still, the imposter waited for the drugs to wear off, and when they did, the inner bully started its barrage of attacks. I started to doubt my worthiness again, and I began to fear that Angelina would eventually realize that she could do much better, and would leave me the way the women of my past had done so many times.

After a few more years, I started to feel safer and more worthy. I mean, she was still here, and all the others had left by now. Maybe this was different. Maybe I was worthy of a committed loving romantic relationship. I realized I was learning how to love me the way she did and thus was learning how to love me the way the Universe does. After a few more years, workshops and meditation practice, I brought these thoughts of worthiness from my head into my heart. It is said that *the longest journey we will ever take is from the head to the heart* and I was starting to make this journey in a profound way. Here I was actually beginning to love myself the way the Universe did.

Whenever we can practice loving ourselves by recognizing our beauty, innocence, perfection and unconditional deservedness, we will begin to experience the **Consciousness of Love** that **God/Source/Universe** has for us and that is *the bliss and awareness that our hearts and psyches are ultimately longing for.* **Play track 5-Love Me the Way You Do**

Love me the way you do

Lyrics Armand Della Volpe,
Music Armand Della Volpe and Don Rowell

I look onto your face, the sun beats down on you,
It makes me warm and high inside,
But then I see an even brighter shade of blue,
When I look into your eyes,
You're more than all I ever wanted in someone,
You bring me love I never knew,
I'm here to help you know you've always been enough,
I devote my life to you.
If I could only love me the way you do,
If I could only love me the way you do,
I'd breathe in all the beauty that wakes me up to life,
Wakes me up to life, wakes me up to you.

You say you love me as you look into my soul,
I find it so hard to believe,
But what I love is just a mirror of myself,
Look at what you've done for me.

I'm learning how to love me the way you do,
I'm learning how to love me the way you do,
I'm breathing all the beauty that wakes me up to life,
Wakes me up to life, wakes me up to you.

Happiness is simply learning how to love,
It's more abundant than the grains of sand,
Unless we open up and give it to ourselves,
It'll slip right through our hands.

There's still a part of me that doesn't have a clue,
Why you say that I'm the one,
'Cause everything you are has drawn my heart to you,
Paradise has just begun.

I finally learned to love me the way you do,
I finally learned to love me the way you do,
I'm breathing all the beauty that wakes me up to life,
Wakes me up to life, wakes me up to you.

CHAPTER TWENTY

Complimenting the Convict for Good Behavior

"The space between you and Home, is only a series of compliments away."
-Matt Kahn

How often do we compliment ourselves? How often do we engage in self-admiration? Society has basically condemned any form of self-admiration as a form of conceit. But this is not the kind of arrogant pride which comes from an excessive sense of self-importance, but is more of a healthy recognition of just how wonderful, amazing and divine we are. As previously stated, we are always doing the best we can. We can't get it wrong, AND we get an A+ with extra credit. If we take this one step further, we can't help but admire our being and shower ourselves with compliments. The trick is always having the awareness that *what makes us so worthy of admiration and compliments is also what makes everyone else equally worthy.* Superiority and Inferiority have no place in our lives if we want to free ourselves from the penitentiary.

Here is a tool that we use to help us get into more self-admiration. We call it a "*compliment list.*" Make it a practice to give yourself at least two compliments per day; preferably in the morning upon rising, and just before bed. This will break the habit of reserving compliments and admiration for others. It can be as simple as saying, "I am doing a great job today of doing this *compliment list.*"

Here's a compliment I gave myself recently. "Today I had the privilege and honor to observe Armand just doing his life. I have not always been there for him, but even though he did not always behave in the most honorable ways, I always knew there was something amazing about him, and I always knew his heart was pure. Today I realized just how much he has survived; from a painful and often abusive childhood, to multiple addictions, to multiple failed relationships, to career challenges, and emotional and physical illnesses. Still, somehow he always chose to get back up and recognize his blessings. He used this positivity to do his recovery work, heal his relationship dramas, get his health back in order and forgive all of his past relationships and life lessons. I really admire him and told him that from now on, I will put him first and if he ever needs me, I will drop whatever I am doing and be there for him."

CHAPTER TWENTY-ONE

Treating the Convict the Way You Would a Child

One practice that Angelina and I use to love ourselves the way The Universe loves us, is to treat ourselves like we would a five year-old child. If Angelina or I are critical or say something negative about ourselves, the other will often ask, "Would you say that to a five year old?" If the answer is no, then we take it back and say and think something different. You would be amazed at how often you say and think horrible things about yourself that you would never dream of saying to or even thinking about a five-year-old. Why? Because you know that a five-year-old is a beautiful innocent child. You know that what that child needs most is love, appreciation and acceptance. Well guess what? You too are an innocent child of the Universe. You too deserve and need love, appreciation and acceptance from yourself most.

This is not just a practice; it is an obvious result of the consciousness of recognizing our inherent worth and beauty. The next time you say or think something critical about yourself, I encourage you to actually take a step back and remember about whom you are talking. There is a beautiful innocent child in there who wants more than anything for you to recognize his or her beauty, heart and innocence. All the validation that you have sought from others has been a poor substitute and will never satisfy what your innocent child has really been craving, which are pure acceptance, love and appreciation from you.

CHAPTER TWENTY-TWO

Faith in the System

"Everything will be okay as soon as you are okay with everything.
And that's the only time everything will be okay."
-Michael Singer

F.A.I.T.H. has been said to stand for **F**eeling **A**lright **I**n **T**he **H**eart. Feeling alright in the heart does not mean we always understand everything. It doesn't mean we don't get confused. It just means that we trust that, as John Lennon said, "Everything Will Be OK in The End." Being confused is OK. Thinking that there is something wrong with us for being confused is the problem. As Byron Katie says, *"How do I know it was meant to happen that way? Because it did." or "Never argue with reality."*

The more we allow ourselves to feel our feelings, the more faith we have. The more we meditate and quiet the mind, the more faith we have. The less we numb out or medicate, the more faith we have. The less we entertain the voices in our heads, the more faith we have. The more we forgive ourselves and all of life, the more faith we have. The more we remember that everything is happening exactly the way it is supposed to happen, the more faith we have. Again, two things cannot occupy the same space at the same time. We get to choose between faith and fear in each given moment.

In the movie ***The Best Exotic Marigold Hotel,*** the young innkeeper always has an air of faith that no matter what happens, everything will work out. Whenever any of the residents complains to him, he always responds, "We have a saying here in India, '*Everything will be alright in the end, so if it's not alright, it is not yet the end.*'" **Play track 6-OK in The End.**

OK in the end

By Armand Della Volpe

Everything will be OK in the end; if it's not OK, it's not the end (*repeat*)

Nothing in this Universe will ever last,

So if you're feeling low, this too shall pass (*repeat*)

Everything will be OK in the end; if it's not OK, it's not the end (*repeat*)

Sha la la la la, sha la la la la la (*repeat*)

Even when the darkness seems to hide your way,

After every night, a brand new day (*repeat*)

Everything will be OK in the end; if it's not OK,
it's not the end (*repeat*)

Sha la la la la, sha la la la la la (*repeat*)
Even when it all just seems to go your way,
Don't get attached, it's gonna change. (*repeat*)

Everything will be OK in the end; if it's not OK, it's not the end (*repeat*)

It's not the end…….it's not the end (*repeat*)
But this is the end.

CHAPTER TWENTY-THREE

Why the System Needs Us?

"There never has been an expression of God that is any greater than you."
-Goofball Guru

The Universe needs YOU. God is expressing itself through you in a way that cannot happen through anyone else.

Really!

You are no less valuable than any of the greatest people who ever lived.

True!

You provide a *flavor/color/character* that without you would not get fulfilled.

Absolutely!

Like any other piece of a puzzle, without you, the puzzle is not complete.

Word!

Do you see how **important, valid and amazing** you are? Do you see how **important, valid and amazing** everyone else is? **See why the Universe needs YOU**?

CHAPTER TWENTY-FOUR

The Wiseman from Alcatraz

"There's so much beauty in the world, I feel like I can't take it, and my heart is just going to cave in"
-from the movie American Beauty

Every time I watch the musicals, ***Jesus Christ Superstar, Phantom of the Opera, Wicked*** or ***Beauty and the Beast,*** I am moved and feel more connected with all of humanity. These are stories about love, hate, devotion, betrayal, faith, hopelessness, healing, torture, beauty, government corruption, charity, wealth inequality, forgiveness and ultimately, about surrender. Does this remind you of anything? How about Planet earth? How about our lives? I have often wondered why so many of us feel so peaceful, inspired and connected after watching these shows filled with such tragedy and darkness; yet, even miniscule similar occurrences in our personal lives can send us into an emotional/mental tailspin. It's all about judgment.

When we watch the characters in movies and shows, we don't judge them. We see them as playing the part they were scripted to play. We don't try and change them. We simply get moved by their performances. If we are truly open, then we see them in ourselves and us in them. This kind of *empathy will always bring us more peace and connection, while judgment always brings us more pain and separation.*

We can do this with our personal lives as well, but as I said earlier, we will have to create some space between what we observe and the *One* that is observing. This observing one is also called "the watcher." Eckhart Tolle calls it "disidentifying from the ego." Billy Shakespeare said, **"All the world's a stage, and all the men and women merely players. They have their exits and their entrances, and one man in his time plays many parts."** From a place of observation, we connect with our true eternal being and don't get enmeshed with the human drama and our human selves. Instead we feel appreciation and pure acceptance for the part we and others are playing. Our **human self** may get triggered by the events, but our **observer Self** is just fascinated by the whole show. Since we do have influence over our character, we can choose to do some rewrites and coach our character from a very clear and unemotional place, but we don't try and change any of the other actors. We also don't beat ourselves up for parts we played in the past since we know that we did exactly as we were scripted to do then.

Back in 2014, I was struggling with yet another relationship challenge. A dear friend and I had had a blow up and we both ended up in what Greg Baer calls *"the field of death."* I said lots of things that were judgmental as well as taking much of what they said personally, which totally violated my inner parole. The relationship ended painfully and I felt embarrassed and like I failed… AGAIN!

> During meditation, I pleaded to Creator, "Why do I keep messing up in situations like this?"

The answer I got was surprising, "BECAUSE YOU ARE A GOOFBALL GURU".

> "Umm, what? I mean I know I mess up from time to time but not sure I am as much of a goofball as many others I know."

"YOU ONLY THINK THAT WAY SO YOU CAN FEEL SUPERIOR."

> "OK, I get that. Yes, everyone messes up, and that is the human condition; we all do the best we can. Well, what about the guru part? I mean I know I have some wisdom at times but I am not a guru like my heroes Eckhart Tolle, Paramahansa Yogananda, Buddha and Jesus, right?"

"YOU ONLY THINK THAT WAY SO YOU CAN FEEL INFERIOR."

Wow! That hit me like a ton of bricks. From then on I started calling myself The Goofball Guru for it kept me from feeling inferior or superior.

The next time you feel triggered by something, take a deep breath and try and create some space between you and the event. You can close your eyes and bring your attention to the "third eye" between your eyebrows, or even physically lean back as Michael Singer suggests in his book *The Untethered Soul.* You will be amazed at how much more enjoyable LIFE is when we are fascinated with our observation of the world versus being all caught up in the drama. I will repeat what I stated in Chapter 20. *Superiority and Inferiority have no place in our lives if we want to free ourselves from the penitentiary.*

CHAPTER TWENTY-FIVE

No-one is Responsible (Guilty). Everyone is Accountable

I first heard, "We are not responsible for what we do," from Eckhart Tolle in his groundbreaking book *The New Earth.* He claims that when we do negative things, it is merely our *pain body* that has taken over. This resonated deeply in my soul even though I had held the "self-responsible" position my whole life. It was only when I embraced my innocence that I was capable of fully embracing "non-responsibility." The word "responsible" is a very loaded word. One definition is... **Being the primary cause of something, and so able to be blamed or credited for it.** This is a great way to perpetuate judgment, shame and guilt, which have plagued most of us for decades. So, like it or leave it, here is the cure for all of that... **Stop making you and others the primary cause of everything, so you no longer are able to blame or give credit for it!** Instead, trust that everything is divinely scripted. Hold **The Universe** responsible for everything, and let yourself and everyone else off the judgmental hook!

What if time was not linear? What if you were merely reviewing a past that already occurred thinking you could change it? What if the idea of responsibility was just the **Ego's** way of **Edging God Out?** Can you truly surrender to a higher power? Do you believe "It's all in Divine Order," or are you like most, offering lip service to a teaching that you can't truly embrace? I sure know what that's like; I've done it for decades.

OK, now that you are probably breaking out in a cold sweat, I want to buffer things a bit with the word *accountable.* It is often used as a synonym. However, you will rarely hear anyone use the word to put someone down. We call people and actions irresponsible, but we don't say that someone or their actions are not accountable. Instead, it is more of a "what goes around comes around" type of concept. If we believe that "The All is One and the One is All" and "We always get back what we put out," then of course, everything is connected. Thus, there will be consequences/accountability for everything. That doesn't mean responsibility. Accountability is a given but Responsibility is very subjective. Is the tree responsible or irresponsible for dropping seeds, dying or uprooting your driveway? Nope. Still, there will be consequences and accountability. Is a baby responsible for throwing up on your new clothes? Nope, but there will be consequences. **I don't believe you, I, anyone who has ever hurt us, or anyone else is solely responsible for "what is." I believe in a Divine Order/God/Goddess/Eternal Presence/Higher Power/Universe that is ultimately responsible for everything. Now, that doesn't mean that we don't make apologies and amends. It's just as I said earlier… when we remove the guilt and responsibility, making amends becomes a joyous heavenly adventure into personal evolution.

CHAPTER TWENTY-SIX

Getting Our Drugs into the Jailhouse

Everyone wants to feel good. One of the most important aspects of how we feel is based upon the chemicals that run through our nervous system. **This is way beyond my area of expertise, but I will share what I believe to be the simplest and most important information. For simplification purposes, let's call them "*happy drugs" and "unhappy drugs.*" When we are happy, our body produces chemicals in our brains that magnify our experience. These chemicals have fancy names like oxytocin, serotonin, dopamine, etc. The same is true when we are sad, angry or frustrated.

The challenge is that these chemicals are also produced by our unconscious minds. We can be experiencing happiness about an event, etc. and our bodies can still be producing chemicals that feel bad to us based upon an unconscious feeling of unworthiness or an old painful event that the current event is triggering. How many times have we consciously loved how life was showing up for us, but we still did not feel joyous?

Here are a few ways to trigger the body into producing more "*happy drugs.*" Through scientific methods, it is possible to measure the brain activity and see what is going on in there.

1. **Generosity** - When we are generous, our brains *produce "happy drugs."* There is a catch though. We must have no expectations of receiving anything in return. This expectation could actually produce the opposite if we don't get back what we want, causing us to feel resentment and disappointment as well as thwarting the initial chemicals because we are not fully giving from a generous heart and mind.

2. **Appreciation** - Our brains also produce *"happy drugs"* when we are truly grateful for what we have, what we are experiencing or for life itself. One effective way to trigger this feeling is to do a gratitude list. Many spiritual teachings, including ***12 Step Work in The Anonymous Programs*** incorporate the use of *gratitude lists.* You will be amazed at how doing these lists can trigger joy and appreciation, and result in more good feelings. The most powerful time to do a *gratitude list* is when you are having trouble feeling good. This is not the easiest time to do this, but it is really effective.

3. **Petting Animals** (friendly animals of course) - When we pet our animals, our brains give us more *"happy drugs."* Our own pets, the pets of others and petting zoos are an excellent source of these *"happy drugs."* Studies have also shown that our pets experience these *"happy drugs"* as well.

4. **Engaging in Life Enhancing Pursuits** - Exercise, yoga, meditation, being in nature, entertainment, get-togethers with friends, rest, etc. all can inspire the brain to produce more *"happy drugs."* The trick is to make sure we find balance as overdoing some of these pursuits can become addictive, which will magnify any unworthiness and sabotage our joy and happiness.

CHAPTER TWENTY-SEVEN

How I Adjusted My Life Sentence

*"It is said that there are three ways we can change something that is destined to happen to us. One is with **prayer**, the second is by **giving charity**, and the third is by **changing our ways**. The most powerful is the last. There are destinies we can undo when we make the effort to sincerely transform our negative attributes."*
-Daily Kabbalah *from Karen Berg*

In the movie, ***The Adjustment Bureau***, Matt Damon's character was able to break free from where his life was surely fated, into a new more powerful **destiny.** This brought up many questions for me regarding Destiny, Fate, what can be changed and what cannot. This is what came to me in meditation.

It appears that some life sentences are unchangeable, and some are not. Let's just look at the changeable sentences. **Fate** is what shows up for us if we keep doing what we've always done. **Destiny** is what shows up when we are willing to break free from our patterns and step into a whole new consciousness. Moving from fate to destiny requires discipline and surrender. Addiction and Recovery work like 12-Step Anonymous programs are a great example of how one's fate can be changed.

When one is an addict, that person is fated to act out as an addict for the rest of his/her life. Fortunately, that does not have to be that person's destiny. By looking beyond the current fated reality into an empowered promise of sobriety, the addict can move beyond the control of addiction into a new freedom and destiny.

I personally believe that I was sentenced to *fail at romantic partnership as a result of addiction and a feeling of unworthiness.* I believe that I was sentenced to *have a heart attack by my 55rd birthday.* I believe that I was sentenced to *feel small around my surrogate mother.* All of these have been adjusted. By the Grace of God and lots of prayer, meditation, discipline and compassion for myself and others, I have managed to **allow conscious committed romantic partnership to flourish in my life while simultaneously conquering my addictions**. I also managed to **divert a heart attack through changing my diet, adding supplements, taking a pharmaceutical and keeping my emotional heart open.** In addition, **I no longer feel small relative to my Sacred Villain, who I now know was actually a part of The Universe's Conspiracy upon My Behalf.**

There is much more I get to learn and heal, but that's just a few ways I believe I have adjusted my sentence of **fate** to embrace my **destiny**. Then again, all of that may have been pre-destined as well. ***The Universe is certainly a tricky One.***

CHAPTER TWENTY-EIGHT

Trying to Escape Prison While We Are Still Shackled

I am continually amazed at how everything is working toward Consciousness. As a Kriya Yoga disciple, I am committed to full Self/God Realization. I would like it to be this lifetime too, but I am not attached. Over and over again I have experienced some really painful relationship karma. One minute, I'd be high as a kite, flying through life like never before, and then, in an instant I'd fly smack dab into a mountain. The message I got one morning during meditation helped me to understand this in a much more simple, yet joyous way.

Imagine that we are like a butterfly that goes through many stages until our wings are fully developed and we reach ***"Butterfly Enlightenment."*** At this point we would be able to fly anywhere available with ease, peace and joy. Now, what if you are a butterfly like me and are always exploring higher possibilities? *If we try and fly higher than our wings can handle, someone or some experience will painfully put us back down to our level of consciousness.* At this point we can either stay down, which would have the symptoms of blame, resentment, victim, attack and making the other person or situation wrong. Or, we can return to the cocoon, feel the pain fully, forgive everything involved and see where the pain is leading us. If we do that, then we will grow stronger, more conscious wings, and be able to fly higher than before.

We then can be grateful to the people and experiences that have inspired us, often through force and pain, to go back into the cocoon of higher consciousness so we can continue to become a more powerful butterfly. We often curse them at first because it hurts, but it has become abundantly clear what a gift they are to us and humanity.

SECTION VII

Stepping Out of the Prison Gates

CHAPTER TWENTY-NINE

Time to Fire the Jury and Pardon Ourselves

"A day will come when you will be stirred by unexpected events. A part of you will die and you will begin to search for the elixir that will bring this part of you back to life. You will seek the elixir in friends, lovers, enemies, books, religions, foreign countries, heroes, songs, rituals and jobs, but no matter where you look the treasure will evade you.

All will seem lost and you will lose all hope that this magic potion even exits. This will be the darkest of nights and this promise of certain death will lead you to the abyss of despair. But staring into the abyss you will see the dim light of your own illuminated soul.

Your radiance will transform the abyss into the elusive elixir of life and for the first time you will realize that all the while it is your own light that you've been searching for."

- *Growing into Grace* by Mastin Kipp

There comes a time when we need to fire the jury. We can do this with outside people and especially need to do so with the juries/voices in our heads. This doesn't mean we have to disown anyone or any parts of ourselves. Instead, we must no longer allow any voices to decide our fate or innocence. When we embrace our inherent beauty and perfection, we essentially pardon ourselves for all the false confessions and/or imposed guilt. This will truly feel like we are being released from a prison; yet most of us don't even recognize we are in a self-imposed prison until we start to get free.

CHAPTER THIRTY

Presenting the Statute of Limitations

"If you don't believe in reincarnation, you will in your next lifetime."
-Swami Beyondananda

Do we ever consciously regret or feel sorrow or remorse for anything we did in a past lifetime? I rather doubt it. Whether we believe in reincarnation or not, none of us consciously beat ourselves up for what we may or may not have done in our past lifetimes. That was another time, another character and another set of circumstances. We can have this same acceptance for anything we have done in our past in **this** lifetime. Imagine how wonderful life would be if we just accepted that everything we ever did was the best we could at the time, without giving energy to how we could have done it differently. Instead, that time and energy could be spent on making this now moment and even the future better by gratefully acknowledging how our new wisdom will help us evolve into an even greater version of ourselves. As Rafiki said in *The Lion King*, "The past can hurt. But the way I see it, you can either run from it or learn from it." Either way, we must never blame ourselves for it.

CHAPTER THIRTY-ONE

10 Principles For Self-Parole

*"We will experience the New Earth when our Higher **Self** is able to love the living shit out of our human **self**."*
-Goofball Guru

1. We Are All One. Nothing happens to any of us without it happening to All of Us.

2. Trust in an Infinite Intelligence that is orchestrating All of Life.

3. Thou shalt not argue with what is. Make nothing wrong.

4. Take quiet time each day to relax and reflect upon your infinite innocent nature. This nourishes the soul.

5. Completely forgive your parents, yourself, everyone and everything by fully embracing that things could not have happened any other way than they did. Herein lies the Peace of God/Goddess/Spirit.

6. Thou shalt not disrespect anyone's belief/religion. All beliefs/religions are imagined/made up, so each deserves equal respect.

7. Be completely content with what you have. By doing this, you will always feel abundant.

8. Speak **your** truth. When **your** truth changes, be quick to humbly admit it. We all have the right to change our minds. Do your best to only say things that are kind and/or necessary and timely.

9. Revel in everyone's good fortune. This brings good fortune into your experience. Do not pity others for this brings pain into your experience. You cannot know why another is experiencing anything.

10. Practice the Art of Gratitude for Life itself and all its facets. A Grateful Life is a Happy Life.

CHAPTER THIRTY-TWO

Time to Pardon Our Sacred Villains

"My spiritual teachers in order of importance.
The people that annoy the living shit out of me.
All other spiritual teachers."
-anonymous

My most challenging and painful teacher has always been my surrogate mother. I call our most challenging people ***Sacred Villains***. When my mom and dad divorced and my mom went away, another female became the closest to a mother I had. Even though my father was an amazing parent and also assumed much of the mothering responsibility, I still projected more mothering identity onto my surrogate mother. I have been working on forgiving her off and on for over 20 years. Each time I forgave her more, I felt better and more connected. A few years ago, I got to a deeper level of forgiveness, which included immense gratitude. Here's what came to me...

This woman was willing to be abusive: physically, mentally and emotionally to me and mirror my own self-abuse in order to inspire me to evolve into the man I am today. She was willing to suffer the rejection and hatred that I felt for her many times in my life. She was even willing to suffer the rejection that she received from her own mother for the way she treated me. Her mother went so far as to not allow her to come and visit her for the last five years of her life. Even with all of this, she continued to offer me the treatment that my soul demanded from her.

What a sacrifice! What a gift to me! What a soul sister! My hope for her is that she can fully forgive herself for all of the abuse. I love you dear Teacher/Sacred Villain/Christ.

CHAPTER THIRTY-THREE

How I Got Off of Death Row and Cured My Depression

Could inner peace and happiness be as simple as feeling innocent and lovable? I was starting to believe that it was. Back in 2011, when I finally let myself feel all my feelings, I slipped into what felt like "depression." I now see it more as «*a full recognition of how scared, angry, and unlovable I felt*» or ***"deep expression."*** I could have taken the advice of many and gone the psychiatric/pharmaceutical route. I could also have, at any time, numbed out again like I had done so many times before, but I chose to just be with all of it. This was super hard on Angelina, but she supported me fully. We had some savings to cover the bills for about eight months, so we were OK.

This lasted about five months until I was hurting enough to take a **course in *Vipassana Meditation*.** This would be a ten day silent instructional meditation course that involved **ten hours a day of meditation**. I was truly alone. **This rocked my world!**

This course brought decades of fears, anxiety, pain, anger, vindictiveness and hopelessness to the surface. **It also gave me awareness and insights as to *my true innocent, lovable, worthy nature* that I hadn't felt since early childhood. ***This intrinsic nature did not need attention, women, spirituality or career to be present.*** I felt my attachment to all of my drugs begin to diminish. I even felt a healthy non-attachment to Angelina. I wanted to just stay at the retreat center forever. I had never felt this good about myself and I was afraid to lose it. Still, I needed to go home, face my world and find a way to incorporate my new peace and lovability into my relationship and life. Re-entry at home was extremely difficult. I wanted to be alone to process my new awareness's with little regard for how it would affect Angelina. After two weeks of disconnection, Angelina and I found a new groove and became even more connected and loving toward each other than ever before. She noticed that I was more at peace and began to feel even more loved, cherished and respected by me.

Vipassana is the most powerful technique that I have found that works this way for me. It requires daily practice to continue to allow the darkness to be released and keeps me aware of my beautiful, lovable self.

Shortly after Vipassana, Angelina and I were initiated into Kriya Yoga by the Rev. Ron Lindhan at the Center for Spiritual Awareness in Northern Georgia, founded and led by Roy Eugene Davis. This practice incorporates meditation, yoga, exercise, healthy eating, loving-kindness, rest, time in nature, and telling the truth about oneself. As I engage in these practices, I remind myself that I am lovable and worthy of peace and happiness. Again, I have more loving-kindness to share with others.

I feel that my emptying, awareness and new practices have cured me of my "deep expression" (anxiety and depression), and I plan to spend the rest of my life becoming more and more awake to what is real and true. This doesn't mean that sadness and anxiety won't rear their ugly heads again. It just means that I will no longer go where they try and lead me and I will never feel hopeless again. Ram Dass once said something like this, *"I still have all of my neuroses. The difference is now when I hear them knocking. I invite them in for a quick drink before I show them the door."*

CHAPTER THIRTY-FOUR

UHGS Unconditional Happiness and Gratitude Society

"If you decide that you're going to be happy from now on for the rest of your life, you will not only be happy, you will become enlightened. Unconditional happiness is the highest technique there is. This is truly a spiritual path and it is as direct and sure a path to Awakening as could possibly exist."
-Michael A. Singer

I founded UHGS in 2013 when I decided to get sober from unhappiness. I had conquered most of my physical addictions and had made great strides in healing my co-dependency. Now it was time to go even deeper. **I had been addicted to unhappiness,** and 50 years of that addiction was more than enough. So I took a ***"white chip,"*** which represented my commitment to staying sober from unhappiness no matter what. This was not pretending to be happy like I did when I was a "bliss bunny," by hiding from the painful thoughts and emotions through a façade of positive thinking. This was a decision to choose unconditional happiness no matter what. I didn't expect perfection, and I knew it was just

"one day at a time." Still, this was the next right thing to do for me and as I kept my focus and discipline on Sobriety, I was more and more able to conquer this *dis-ease* just as I did with the many others.

This unhappiness I speak of is not the circumstantial unhappiness that most of us think of, but the unwillingness to feel peaceful, accepting and content with whatever shows up in any situation. I know that one of the keys to unhappiness sobriety is to allow all feelings, thoughts and emotions that I have, to run their course without allowing myself to believe that they are me. I may have a sad thought or emotion, but just like how I have a body, they are not me. I may be involved in a relationship that has issues, but it's not me. I may have a car that needs repair, but it's not me. I may have character flaws in my personality but my personality is not me. As Michael Singer says, "It all comes down to choice. You either choose to be happy or not." The same is true of any addiction. You either choose sobriety or you choose to act out. Whether the thoughts are consciously or unconsciously driving the addiction, we still have the choice to say NO!

As I digested all the amazing spiritual, emotional and mental tools that I had discovered, taught and practiced over the years, I realized that along with gratitude, happiness was also a choice. What if every time we started to feel ungrateful or unhappy, we reminded ourselves of our innocence and worthiness? What if every time we started thinking things should be different, we reminded ourselves that The Universe, like us, can't get it wrong? Gratitude and happiness are the natural result of this knowing. It takes practice though… just like any other form of sobriety, the old compulsion will show up.

Here is a tool that I use to help me stay in the vibration of happiness and gratitude. I call it a **grati2wee** / gradɢ'to͞oé/, and it rhymes with *ratatouille.* A grati2wee is when we follow up any complaint or negative thought with two things or thoughts you are grateful for around the same situation.

Here's an example. Let's say you are driving and someone cuts you off. Your knee-jerk response may be, "What an idiot! I can't believe they did that to me." You can follow that up with, "I am grateful they did not hit me," and "I am grateful that I don't have to be in a car with them." Immediately, you will feel better.

The minute you go into a complaint and judgment, you have lowered your vibration. At that time, you can both spiral down and stay where you are, or you can actually raise your vibration to a place higher than it was before the event happened. If you have a partner, you can remind each other to do a grati2wee. Sometimes you may get so triggered and stuck, you are just not in the space to do a grati2wee. At this time it can be helpful to invite your partner to do one for you.

As I mentioned earlier, we can look at our life as if it were a movie. I would say that we are generally happy when we watch movies regardless of what the content of the movie is. Yes, we allow our emotions to flow and respond to scenes, but we don't absorb the emotions into our overall being. We know everyone is just acting and that the director and writer set it all up to give us that experience. What if our entire human lives were just an elaborate movie? We are playing our parts. Everyone else is playing their parts. That doesn't mean we don't show up fully. It just means that our true eternal nature is the one behind the scenes watching it all in enjoyment and fascination. When we tap into that part of ourselves, we too can stay unconditionally happy and grateful for our lives.

Back in July of 2003, Angelina was plucking on her classical guitar the chords to Beethoven's 9th Symphony and telling me how grateful she was. I reminded her that speaking gratitude is really powerful, but singing it would be like praying twice. She said, "You mean you think I should write a song? I've never written a song before." I reminded her that anything truly great that had ever been done was done by someone who had never done it before. She immediately began to sing along with Ludwig's melody, and voila! She had written her first lyrics to a song. **Play track 7-Ode to Gratitude**

Ode to Gratitude

Lyrics Angelina, music Beethoven

I am grateful, oh so grateful for the blessings in my life,

I am grateful, oh so grateful for the blessings in my life,

Thank you Spirit, O Great Spirit, omnipresent in all things.

I am grateful, oh so grateful for the blessings in my life.

CHAPTER THIRTY-FIVE

Keys to Freedom by Reviewing the Evidence

1. We were born as an original blessing.
2. We are always ENOUGH... Period!
3. We always do the best we can at any given moment.
4. There is no way to make the wrong decision.
5. No one is better or more worthy of love than anyone else.
6. The more you appreciate and/or accept all of life, the better you feel.
7. There is no right or wrong/good or bad, only consequences.
8. We are at the only place we can be right now.

CHAPTER THIRTY-SIX

The Verdict…
aka Here Comes the Judge

So here we are, a part of the tapestry of the Universe, playing our parts perfectly and divinely. We have more than enough evidence to convince any jury of our innocence. There are very few limits to our capabilities. There are, however, some absolute limitations. No matter how hard we try, it is impossible for us to be unlovable. It is equally impossible for us to get it wrong. Who's tried? I know I have! It is absolutely impossible for us to be anything less that the divine, eternal, worthy, innocent beings we have always been. Thus, it is ultimately impossible for us to ever be truly convicted of not being "enough." In that case, an acquittal of our original case is inevitable.

I Now Pronounce Us All…Not Guilty!!!

Play track 8-Innocent

Innocent

By Armand Della Volpe

I heard about this young kid, who served his prison time,

For a crime he did not do.

He gave a false confession, and when they asked him why, he said I did not know the truth…he was innocent.

I thought about my own life, how I was like that kid, when they told me I was bad, I gave a false confession, to what they said I did and lost the childhood I once had.

I am innocent, I did nothing wrong, I've been serving time for this crime for far too long. I am not to blame for what I didn't do; there is nothing I need to prove. I am innocent.

This is the time for justice, this time we'll get it right, we're finally hearing the whole truth. I fired all my juries and got the pardon I deserved and now I'm freeing other inmates too.

You are innocent, you did nothing wrong, you've been serving time for this crime for far too long. You are not to blame for what you didn't do; there is nothing you need to prove.

We are innocent, we did nothing wrong, we've been serving time for this crime for far too long. We are not to blame for what we didn't do; there is nothing we need to prove.
We are innocent.

FREEDOM

ABOUT THE AUTHOR

Armand has been an inspirational speaker and spiritual musician since 1997. His music has been featured on several episodes of TV shows, used as theme music, and his articles have had magazine publication as well. He was ordained as a minister by The Universal Brotherhood Movement in 2000, and has spoken and performed at over 400 churches, spiritual centers, conferences and events. His music has also been featured on several radio programs as well as Music Choice. He is also a spiritual counselor who reminds his clients of their innocence.

He has been romancing and performing with his wife and life-partner Angelina since 2001, which he lovingly refers to as his bride. They were legally married at Planet Hollywood Chapel in Las Vegas, Nevada in 2011.

They have over ten professionally produced music CDs ranging from meditation and Native American flute instrumentals, to Rock Opera vocal productions. Armand and Angelina travel over 250 days a year speaking, performing and teaching at spiritual centers, churches and events. They have performed with Marianne Williamson, Neale Donald Walsh, Alan Cohen, Gregg Braden, Don Miguel Ruiz, Dan Millman, Joan Borysenko, Mary Morrissey and Patti Cota Robles.

www.armandandangelina.com

https://www.facebook.com/armandandangelina